GESTURES & COUNTERPOINTS

BY THE SAME AUTHOR

GESTURES & COUNTERPOINTS

POEMS

JOHN MOLE

Shoestring Press

Printed by imprintdigital
Upton Pyne, Exeter
www.digital.imprint.co.uk

Typesetting and cover design by narrator
www.narrator.me.uk
info@narrator.me.uk
033 022 300 39

Published by Shoestring Press
19 Devonshire Avenue, Beeston, Nottingham, NG9 1BS
(0115) 925 1827
www.shoestringpress.co.uk

First published 2017
© Copyright: John Mole
© Copyright author photograph: Benjamin Mole
© Copyright cover illustration, "Rain": Mary Norman

The moral right of the author has been asserted.

ISBN 978-1-910323-76-2

ACKNOWLEDGEMENTS

Some of the poems in this volume first appeared in the following publications:

Agenda, Allegro, The Charles Causley Society Newsletter, The European English Messenger, The Interpreter's House, New Walk, The Rialto, The Shop, The Spectator, Stand, The Times Literary Supplement, The Warwick Review.

ABOUT THE AUTHOR

John Mole's most recent publications are *The Point of Loss* (Enitharmon) and *Treatment* (Shoestring Press) which recounts the side-effects of chemotherapy with 'more power and reality than any information leaflet could ever testify to.' (The Lancet). He has received the Gregory and Cholmondeley Awards, and the Signal Award for his poems for children which Charles Causley welcomed in the TES as 'the work of a true poet.' A keen musician, he has worked as a librettist with several composers, including Bob Chilcott, and plays regularly as a jazz clarinettist.

CONTENTS

THE SOUND OF LADDERS

The rattle and clank of home improvements
as the whole street puts a face on it
and neighbours look out at each other.

Scrape, scrape, scrape. Old white paint
flakes to the pavement like snow.
For the sake of appearances we make it new,

enhance the value of our property
in these difficult times. Good luck to them
says the milkman as he exchanges full

for empty bottles, says the postman
delivering unwanted mail, the circulars,
appeals and credit ratings, the advice

to save online. Remember, if you can afford
a makeover you're worth it but if not
there's still a glamorous net to surf on.

So listen to the sound of ladders going up
to paint a corner of the world
where houses safely bought and sold

know little of what elsewhere would conspire
to bring them down, the turbulence
of discontent, eviction, envy, and a view

from which that ladder leant against the moon
in Blake's engraving shows a tiny figure
gone ahead of two who cling together

watching him as, one foot on a rung,
he starts to climb and cries out fiercely
on behalf of all of us 'I want! I want!'

THE WHOLE THING

Take, for example,
the case of Winston Churchill
when it revealed itself
as the universal mystery
complete with solution:
But it was after dinner
so I let it go.
                  Or Bertrand Russell
when it came up and hit him
as he fell from his bike
and lay there stunned
by the absence of God
before dusting himself off
and journeying on.
                  Or any one of us
in that intimate instant
of joy or despair
that calls the whole thing
uniquely into question
wherever we think we are.

SELLING GERANIUMS

Saturday's unique melancholy
is the dead weight of rain
as we hoist tarpaulin.
It holds. The tubular poles
have slithered and clanked
to an upright stiffness,
and sheltered under this
we shall sell geraniums.

At least what we offer
is a concentration of light,
a dream of window-boxes
to take home from market
for tomorrow. Illusion
clings to its stem, bedded
in earth like this, eloquent
and profuse. It holds.

AGAINST ADVICE

For Veronica Furner

Her apple tree felled
became logs for our fire.
Let them dry out she said
and use them next year.

As I stacked them I noted
their moist, mottled bark
but my usual impatience
soon put them to work.

Reluctant to kindle,
they sizzled and spat
like the right words in waiting
but not ready yet.

Then after a while
smoke turned to flame
and with sudden combustion
the poem came.

EFFIGIES

They lie side by side,
her hand in his,
no hound at their feet
but a restless cat
that prowls the duvet
until it discovers
the crook of his spare
extended arm.

Two effigies, remembering
how they would wake
and turn to each other
when her body allowed,
but visited now
by a phantom embrace
no less in love
than they ever were.

PAIN

'I think there's a pain somewhere in the room,'
said Mrs Gradgrind, 'but I couldn't positively
say that I have got it.' – Charles Dickens, *Hard Times*

It chases its tail
around your body,
and you'll know soon enough
if it's yours,
a stray companion
looking for a home
which chooses you
but cannot settle,

although for a while
its restlessness
may be unfamiliar
like a kitten
gazing up at you
as if you might yet
deny its right
to leap into your lap.

THE WHEELCHAIR LADY

They watched her, there on the beach,
how every fine day in summer
she'd be brought down from the Home
and settled, gazing out to sea. It had been
the sleeping sickness claimed her
many years back, since when she'd lived
in a world that none could enter
or possibly understand. Locked in,
she seemed at peace as holiday-makers
came and went, their children
shrill with a look-at-me excitement
rushing toward the edge, laughing
while playful waves leapt up, making as if
to knock them over. Then suddenly
one small boy, unattended, cried out,
stumbling in the shallows, appeared
to be in trouble, and it seemed nobody
had noticed. Out of her chair
the lady just like a wave leapt up
across the sand to his aid while all around
rushed on the scene, amazed and fearful,
helping the boy and her together
as if this were some miracle
they found themselves a part of.
It was over so quickly, everyone said,
and couldn't be explained. Nor did it
ever happen again. Back in her chair
the lady resumed her gazing
day after day, calmly, uninterrupted,
out to the horizon, perhaps remembering
something that might have happened
in another life or had she dreamt it
for that instant presently awake?

LIGHT

Let there be light, and there was
entirely by chance as it happened
between his sudden concern
and her need to sit down.

Something in the room with them
had been left standing, a shadow
no longer impatient, lengthening
but tenuous, for that moment

caught off-guard by time
encompassed in the simple gesture
of his watchfulness
and their enduring vows.

HILL VILLAGE

For Jane and Jace Morgan

All is still as we remember it,
the plane trees lit from beneath
to a glow of lime and lemon,
someone's daughter at a window
combing her wet hair, the old ones
grounded in shadow, bending
to their disciplines of concentration,
the thump and click of silver balls
biting the dust, a ritual
and communal observance
in this warm enclosure, swallows
threading the campanile's eye
with its great bell silenced
as they skitter through.

In a corner of the square
a teenage congregation clamours
around its hooded perspex booth
where beauty turns from the phone
to watch a simmering admirer
buck the bronco of his bike,
while on a dry stone wall
beside the cemetery gate
two lovers passing through
have helped each other up,
removed their back-packs,
and before the sun goes down
are gathering all of this
to fill their postcards home.

A POLAR CAROL

Ice-locked, gripped by a groaning floe,
fingers numb on my old banjo
as the Northern Lights put on their show.

Snow all around me
and more snow.

From the blinding dazzle of an endless sky
where time has forgotten how to fly
I send you the jewel of a cormorant's eye.

Goodbye, my love,
goodbye, goodbye.

My breath is a wreath, a ghostly ring,
and my song already vanishing
is all I can offer, is everything.

Listen to the silence,
hear it sing.

Dulce in dulci jubilo,
frostbite plucks at my old banjo,
home seems a million years ago

And snow keeps falling
snow on snow.

THE WOLVES OF MEMORY

Loping through thick snow,
fur matted with ice,
they have lost the trace
that led them long ago
from a legendary tale
to this blank page of survival.

Their warm breath freezes
at the touch of air
as they huddle here
with sharp, bewildered faces
grown solemnly pale
and howl and howl and howl.

KICK-START

Memory, the kick-start
of a mower down on petrol
roaring in its shed
then rolling out of it
to clank on gravel
before stopping dead.

Search for the rusty can
pavilioned in cobwebs
where dad left it last
on a high shelf, the one
with your toy ship's
rudder and broken mast.

Think of him, and of how
he did it just like this
before you were born,
another strip to mow,
those grounded continuities,
that sea-green lawn.

NICO

(age 10)

I have your language but will not speak it,
not to you, not least because you think
you own it and would make it mine.
Each word I learn must enter by permission
at a gate marked Private. We conspire
to keep you out. You ask how it is
you deserved this. Ask the words, not me.
Maybe they fear correction, maybe
but I doubt it. The more of them there are
the more they tell me language is power
and that I have it, that silence is golden
only when, like mine, it's a promise
to be withdrawn, a gift I have to offer
or choose not to accept. They tell me
there's no telling what you would have me do
if the gate fell open and I let you in,
and so I keep it locked. The password
changes as each day they give me
more to guard. Together we evade
your inquisition of control, we understand
that it is kindly meant and meet it
with a pale smile and my furtive shrug
of casual shoulders. Somewhere
between love and patience, puzzlement
and fear, the answer I withhold
may greet its question, maybe so,
but word by word, and certainly for now,
I own a secret that is mine to keep.

THE CAP

for AKJ

Train-spotting after school
and still in uniform
I raced up Forty Steps
to avoid the gang, a loner
with my little book,
but they knew I'd be there:
If the cap doesn't fit
don't let him wear it, they cried.

One of them snatched it
and tossed it to another
who held it high
above their laughter:
Give it me back!
but they never do.
Up it went and over
down past the railings.

The 4.15 thundered beneath
in an ash-flecked steam cloud
while they crowded round
to give me a half-nelson
before wandering off,
and my cap lay quietly
still there on the line
as if nothing had happened.

THE BIKE SHEDS

Behind them was always
best behaviour's location
for time off, to be met
in secret by the selves
we wanted to become
and light the future up.

Under a battered overhang
of corrugated iron
we passed the Woodbines
sacramentally around,
a crouching congregation
in the shorts we'd grown out of.

This was where milk-break's
crates of empty bottles
waited to be collected
from our adolescent
interlude, reminding us
that now was not just yet

but would be soon. In class
with smoke on our breath
we conjugated verbs
in the conditional,
and caught each other's eye,
ambiguously happy to be back.

BACKSTAGE

Minder-surrounded
and autograph-hounded,
the great Count Basie,
a blonde on each knee,
will be signing my book
by hook or by crook
to be first in it. *Look*
he exclaims as we
join the line – the three
of us, Tim, Charlie and me –
It's the Glee Club, girls!,
disengaging an arm
to take my pen
as he grins at them,
their beehives, their pearls,
their sweatered breasts,
and they at us
in our would-be
band-boy blazers
on our would-be cool
night out from boarding school.

Thank you, Count
or *Mr. Basie*, so polite,
so very English,
and isn't one of them a dish
and the other
not bad either,
as he signs with a flourish
while neither
loses her balance –

16

which is what he's done
with the music too,
letting each phrase
hang loose, precarious,
then letting it go
to take its chance
against the strictest tempo.

THE HABIT OF MY PIPE

'His pipe… was an integral and active part of the landscape.'
– Ford Madox Ford, *It Was the Nightingale*

Teeth clamped against the stem
and puffing a cloud around me
like the anthropomorphic little engine
in a picture book, I contemplate
the habit of my pipe, that odd tradition
I belong to, a redundant gentlemanly
keeping faith with clubland's
spirit of fair play, and lighting up
in secret now, a sedentary buffer
at his work desk, not to be found
outside the study's sanctum
with his trusty briar. I think of
what it once meant never to be
without it, deep in conversation
with another chap whose smokescreen
was your mirror image, two
stiff upper lips, putting to rights
a world gone to the dogs
as if to let the pipe for a moment
leave your mouth might signify
the end of empire. Or later
in the officers' mess, its bowl
gripped in your fist, the moist stem
making a point or thrust at a chest
with raucous laughter, you kept
each other's spirits up,
the war a game afoot already won
and in the bag, old man, all over,
done and dusted bar the shouting.
Then, after demob, in a prep school
Common Room, with little Latin
and no Greek, you'd hone the stories

of your finest hours to entertain
a shrill platoon of boys in lieu of lessons,
searching for a matchbox in the pocket
of your elbow-patched, tobacco-scented
tweedy jacket, wondering how life
had shrunk to this, a pipe-dream,
memories and a little leather pouch.
Now, at my desk, these images return
like faces in a cloud, a company
of intimate historic ghosts that soon
I shall belong with, so for them
I keep my pipe lit, this addictive
tribute and redemption, remembering too
one teacher never without his
who if caught in a storm would always
twist it round, bowl pointing down, a quick slip
of the tongue accompanied by teeth
and lips to do the trick, to readjust, then,
as a fellow does, continue smoking.

STUDIO PORTRAIT

My uncle in his uniform,
dog-collared, briar
clutched at an angle,
brilliantined hair
with a central parting,
très debonaire.

This could have been central casting
for the role of padre
in a West End show,
his *Now let us pray*
moment, except that he'd left
for war the next day.

He returned to be vicar
of several parishes,
a warrior in mufti,
modest, diligent, but no less
the charmer of that portrait
in his trim battle-dress,

and seldom without
the starched shine
of a collar's halo
around his neck, put on
each morning, still not a little
glamorously worn.

THE INVISIBLE MAN

So easily overlooked
like an open secret
he came and went
without distinction.

He left no foorprints
as he walked away
across the landscape
of an empty page.

If any considered
that he might be missing
they filed a report
then closed the book.

WILBERFORCE

Wilberforce, après
Le point de départ,
Has turned disappearance
Into an art.

The legends are legion
Concerning his fate,
And where he is now
Is an open debate.

Some say that after
A night on the town
He staggered upstairs
And never came down.

Others who favour
Romantic mystique
Say he listened a while
Then forgot how to speak.

Perhaps he went native
And, counting the cost,
Thought as things were
It was best to be lost.

Or found Shangri La
No less than the truth
And now can't escape
From the land of his youth.

Or, like a phantom,
Walked through the wall
Between body and spirit
To nowhere at all.

But I say that Wilberforce
Entered this rhyme
And in its last stanza
Is biding his time.

TIME TO DANCE

Come, let's trip it as we go
On the light fantastic toe,
Metrically adjusting Milton
To Victor Silvester and Jack Hylton,
George Melachrino, Henry Hall,
Joe Loss, Billy Cotton's call
Of *Wakey Wakey, Hokey Cokey*
(Both examples of the troche),
All those dance bands, dad's delight
On precious ten-inch bakelite,
Each in its separate cardboard sleeve,
Labels for memory to retrieve:
Decca, Brunswick, Parlophone,
Spun on his wind-up gramophone,
The needle tip's engaging hiss
And how he and mum would kiss
Before the band began to play
There and then with no delay
To make a dance hall of the room –
Remember this? or That's our tune! –
Stepping out across the floor
Until that hiss returned once more
When the needle left the groove,
Sliding across from ribbed to smooth.
But what about our own dancing days?
Little enough now left to praise.
Strictly between you and me
My lift's not what it used to be.
As for my heel turn and reverse,
How can incompetence get worse?
I know what you'll say before you answer;
John, you never were a dancer,
Stiff as a board, with two left feet,
Right from the start you lost the beat

And, with no balance to recover,
Proved a most unromantic lover.
But now we're this sedentary pair
In our dreams we can dance on air,
Taking our time, quick quick or slow
Whatever we fancy, dos-a-dos,
Free spin, feather step, light as a breeze,
Basic waltz or Viennese,
Foxtrot, Charleston, Tango, Rumba,
You in a little black-dress number,
Me in tails and shiny pumps
My feet no longer leaden lumps.
If you fly with me and hold on tight
We'll top the leader board tonight.

CEZANNE TO MONSIEUR VOLLARD

Hold yourself like an apple.
Does an apple stir and move?

I have prepared the chair myself.
You don't risk falling in the least.

One hundred and fifteen hours
but now I must go back to Aix.

On my return be assured
I shall have made some progress.

Portraiture takes time.
To get the hands just right.

As for the mouth and eyes,
when I have them I shall know.

For now the shirt front pleases me.
I'm not dissatisfied with that.

A PHOTOGRAPH OF MATISSE IN HIS STUDIO

For John Loveday on his 90th birthday

He stands back from the canvas,
one hand on hip, the other
holding out a charcoal-tipped
extended bamboo pole
that covers the distance
between light's entry
and the last provisional
mark he made.

As for light itself
it pours through the window
his canvas stands beside,
flooding the flagstone floor
around a finished
or abandoned portrait
gazing at him
while he works.

This is the continuum
of art, always
to be watched and measured
by what has been achieved
already falling short,
no less an admonition
than the promise
of the next mark made.

A SCRIPT FOR SATIE

> 'I want to compose a piece for dogs, and I already
>   have my décor. The curtain rises on a bone.'
> – Erik Satie

The curtain rises on a bone,
a canine chorus gathers round
then one of them steps out alone
to tell the audience what's been found.

Although his aria sounds off-key,
a mix of growls and whimperings,
we know it's of mortality,
our common dog's life, that he sings.

We come, we go, and in between
we try to please, get told we're good,
until what remains of us, licked clean,
is bone bereft of flesh and blood.

So let us gambol while we may
as fate keeps whispering in our ear
to warn us all that any day
the terminal hangdog will appear.

He passes the bone across the stage.
The young dogs toss and worry it.
Against the dying light they rage
with angry barks then bury it.

The curtain closes on a grave.
The bone is now where bones belong.
The dogs know just how to behave
and exit with a charnel song.

THE SPRINGER SPANIEL

i.m. Charles Causley & Harry Chambers

Well met at The Springer Spaniel,
Harry and Charles and me,
for genial, sharp-tongued gossip,
good food and poetry.

The appeal of the English ballad
to children (don't call them kids),
would we go for a hot meal or salad?
Whose career was on the skids?

Who was in, who was out, with the critics?
Why was Les Murray so huge?
Harry numbered his favourite restaurants
from Arbutus to Café Rouge.

We chatted of Launceston, Calstock,
St. Albans and Plymouth Sound,
pausing to place our orders
and call in another round.

Harry studied the menu board
with a bon viveur's delight
and a grin as wide as the Tamar
as he settled for more than a bite.

Though Charles's choice, I remember,
was rather less nouvelle cuisine,
the three of us tucked in with gusto
and licked our platters clean.

That long and liquid lunchtime
with laughter and fellowship
was for me the enduring highlight
of an all too brief Cornish trip.

Then Charles left us first and now Harry,
as the ballad of life must end,
but I count it my great fortune
that they welcomed me as a friend.

CROSSING THE COURT

Magdalene College, Cambridge
i.m. SH

A newly-honoured Fellow
arm in arm with Eamon
our mutual friend
and his proposer – myself
invited, privileged
to tag along – we crossed the Court
making for Eamon's rooms
and an after-dinner
snifter. Somehow
Wallace Stevens had come up
and the three of us,
knowing by heart
The Emperor of Ice-Cream
called out in unison
Let be be finale of seem
then declaimed the whole of it
from start to finish,
loud enough to wake
the College living and the dead

Let be be finale of seem
as it has now become
too soon for one of us,
so roll the biggest of cigars
and let the lamp affix its beam
of moonlight above the Court
to shine down as it did that night
on poetry's roaring boy,
a genius off duty, relishing
post-prandial mischief,

who rhymed to set the darkness
echoing, to see himself
and weigh for us all
the measure of his gift.

OLD BOY

The quiet in his mind
is a clubroom. Members
rustle *The Times*
and cough, look up
from the obituaries
with disapproval.
Someone is whispering
over there in the corner
in the present tense
and against the rules.
Someone has yet to learn
how memory must fill
a brandy glass, how
time should pass like this
from day to day
without disturbance,
the light outside
being full of noise
and everybody's business
except his. The quiet
in his mind, its mute
exclusive membership
was just the club for him
and so he joined.

OVERHEARD AT A GARDEN PARTY

I'm afraid this seat is reserved for the bishop.
He went to an even better school than I did
and my wife will be joining us in a minute.
She's over there at the teas, queuing up
with the others. You can park yourself here
until she comes. Of course we all need
to take the weight off our feet
on a day like this whoever we are.
Isn't it a grand occasion! So lucky
to have been invited. How do they keep the lawn
looking so trim? You should see ours
what there is of it. A postage stamp
compared to this, hardly room for a tent
let alone a marquee. All the staff
are splendidly discreet, their uniform
is almost so you wouldn't notice. I'd
take them home with me, especially her,
that pretty one there with the vicar.
I wonder what school he went to.
He seems to know what's what.
It's always an advantage to be well-connected.
Charity depends on it. No, as I said
that seat is taken. Look, here comes my wife
and there's the bishop you've kept it
warm for. I'd introduce you
but I'm sure you must be getting on.
Nice to have met you. We're over here,
my lord, please join us if you will.
I think you've already met my wife.

EXCEPT ME

Everybody, it seems, is writing a novel
except me. Have I thought of writing one,
a friend asks, and I tell her she must be joking.
Who hasn't? The aspirational pipeline
is jammed with them, the pull-out supplements
will show you how to, stage by stage,
and where to join a workshop. Novels
are the real thing, three for the price of two
at Waterstones or buy one get one free
in Tesco. High time, she says, to muscle down.
If anyone can do it why not you? The gardener,
the politician's wife, the chat-show host,
the thief, the cook, his lover. Think of your book
alongside theirs, the company you'll keep.
But that, of course, has always been the problem
and my stumbling block, the company I'd choose
and shame by failing. Believe me, I tell her,
I have tried. Opening, overloaded paragraphs
chock-a-block with would-be intricate parentheses
that led me nowhere close to Henry James
but sank beneath their grave solemnity, a spell
of trying to be Hemingway, hard-boiled
in thrall to imitation, laughable enough
to look at now. Who did I think I was
or could be? All those declarative sentences
punching their weight against a wall
of inexperience. Not to mention my attempts
to join the detective agency and soon discovering
that after the shot rings out there has to be
the echo of a motive and a well-wrought plot
to carry off the body. So, I tell my friend, if anyone
can write a novel, consider all those hours

I've spent, and how embarrassing it is for me
to look back on them now. *Not necessarily,*
she laughs, *think about what you've learned
and how you've put it into words. Besides,
at the very least, there must be a poem in that.*

IN WORDS

For Graham Henderson

Asked if what he had written
was based on experience
(had it happened to him?)
he replied *It happened to me
in words*. Which is what
words do. They start things
happening. They are their own
event and consequence,
act out a private life
in public. Every word
must bear the weight
of what it changes,
whether to make a world
or to undo it. Nothing
that happens anywhere
can be innocent of language
ever. *What I have written
I have written* became an error's
epitaph but may yet proclaim
responsibility and courage.
Witness on every page
the worst struck dumb, the best
evolving syllable by syllable
as you shall trust to find it
in the beginning, in the end
and, in a word, the word.

KIND OF BLUE

Fresh paint on the front door
and bold as its brass knocker
I rap for admittance
to my own house, remembering
the time that Miles Davis
on a gig in Paris knew
the number of his room
but not the hotel. Somebody
please answer. I think I live here
but no key fits, I've tried them all.
Now I can see you, the shape
of your silhouette which turns away
from the window, intent
on rearranging furniture
and placing our ornaments
in strange configurations.
The smell of cooking,
ginger, onions and garlic,
promises the start of a dish
we might have shared
as a last supper. Neighbours,
almost familiar, the entourage
of my misplaced arrival,
ask what this is all about
and if you were expecting
visitors, and why I fail
to recognise their cats
that gather round my loafers
ganging up like sidesmen
ready for a gig. So maybe
this is it, and not too late
to pick an opening number,
choose the key, and hope
that one of us at least
remembers where I live.

IMPROVISATIONS

CHALUMEAU

Not to start on a note
but to sound the depths
before it rises, register
the gloss of ebony
like moonlight searching
for a lover's face.

Only then the intimate
intense vibrato
of a single breath
to end in music
as the melody begins
its water song.

OPTIONS

For Margaret

There being this key
insufficiently padded
and therefore, of course,
wouldn't you believe it,
the one most needed
for the clarinet sonata
we've agreed to play,
I consider my options,
whether a gap
is better than a squeak,
how not to miss the beat
and throw you, risking
that fatal trainwreck
where we don't get back
together on the rails.

Oh life, how easy
to make a mess of it
or improvise
to cope with its surprises,
leaving either
swift recovery or silence
stunned and empty
hanging in the air.

THE BEAT

Laying it down at first is easy.
What you do with it is not.
Now and now and now and now
out of movement melodies grow.

The less familiar they sound
the more the beat has welcomed you
from then and then and then
into a measure of your own.

RIFF

Placing a chord just so
between major and minor
as if being neither
there might be imagined
the point of departure,
the lift-off from doubt,
I follow a riff,
its melodic invention,
its certain crescendo,
a coming together
within and without.

BREAK

For Ben

Go for it, a confident
reverberation, resonant
between each stop-chord,
placing the beat exactly
where it falls or risking
double-time, minding
the gap as your invention
steps across. No words
for this, only the release
of rhythm into sound
that lifts us up and keeps
a steadiness in motion
bar by bar, music's language
needing no translation
as we hear it, waiting
to resume the full ensemble
when we take our cue
from where you join us
back on track, a pulse
that throbs on down the line.

A LINE

Taking a line at random,
wondering why I sounded it,
what blue it came from,
whether to alarm
or to console, I hear
the reminiscent whistle
of an old steam engine
either recently departed

41

with the tender of my life
or heading back
to start all over,
cheerfully uncoupled,
with a fresh bright lick of paint.

AGAINST REPETITION

No, I have played it already,
that particular phrase,
and to do so again
would lead us nowhere.

So I listen to you
as we settle ourselves
for provisional music
in search of each other.

THE CHORD

The timing between one wrong note
and another, the chord
mislaid but out there somewhere.

Promises left behind
in an empty house, whoever made them
calling to come home.

We inherit their life
as a song without words,
a loss beyond appeasement

though the opportunity is ours
to keep time, listen and forgive,
to modulate the chord if not to find it.

SPENT

I've run out of juice
says the old poet
alone in a garden
which certainly hasn't.

Every closed bud
will open to a lyric,
every sapling
soon be in full leaf.

Once, he says,
I was green fingered
but now I wait here
at a loss for words.

OUT OF THE BLUE

He's everywhere I am, out walking
at a loss, resentful it seems
of what he takes to be my purpose,
hurrying along beside me
with his angry little steps. Today,
freshly unshaven he's waiting
not to be shaken off, a mustard T-shirt
and a house key hung around his neck.
I'm a psychologist, he tells me
confidentially or as a spook might say
I know where you live. My cue
to smile with alarm, to offer small talk
as I try to match his pace then slow
in hope he'll race ahead and go on
talking to the air. Instead, with mockery
or a courteous madness, it's the same
each time we meet, as if his pain
has had enough of me and fixed its sights
elsewhere. He turns to shake my hand,
walks on, then turns again not to come back
but to shout with a fierce intensity of parting
Don't expect things to get better!

LAST HOURS IN THE STUDIO

St. Ives

The jet black lining of a silver cloud.
A fuse of light around the full eclipse.

Sand on the sill. An hour glass emptying.
Threadbare curtains lifted by the wind.

The harbour gathering distance in its arms.
The ocean streaming through a needle's eye.

*

His door hangs open. Angled as it was
when he arrived, it starts to close.

His book face down. All reading done
he's ready for departure with the tide.

His bed made up. He rests his case
where age and expectation lie together.

*

Children scattering along the shoreline.
Silence folding its wings above their cries.

Words going on like this without him.
Language doing whatever language can.

Easel and canvas standing by the window.
Darkness waiting as the sun goes down.

DOWNPOUR

Crossing waste ground, three women
join hands in the rain
and, as one, leap over a puddle

as if sprung from some larger chain
they might be the unreported
missing link of, each of them

gloriously wet through. Racing ahead
to a makeshift shelter, the news
not having reached them yet, they

lift up their candid, shining faces
unmasked, leaping over and over,
just being together, loving the rain.

A DIFFERENT LIGHT

The church was full. Light fell
through stained glass, wrapped the aisle
in a cloak of many colours, laying out
a patchwork on the tiles. Already
there was music in the warp and weft
of expectation, threaded string by string
through what we'd come to hear, the long-awaited
lunchtime concert by a local cellist
back from an international career
to play for us. He'd brought the family,
his wife, twin daughters, drowsy bundles
in a double push-chair, safely silent
as the piece began, the warm legato pulse
of Messiaen, his *Praise to the Eternity*
of Jesus lifted by a cello's resonance
above the piano's chords, for little ones
a lullaby, for us the adult wonder
that we'd come to hear.
                              So concentration
bowed our heads, until the closing *sostenuto*
moved us towards silence on the held note
of a prayer, then suddenly out of the mouths of babes
a loud cry joined it, one, and then a second
woken by the first, their counterpoint
a fierce exchange, falsetto, agitated,
not to be appeased. We looked up
as the cellist's closed eyes opened,
widened with an alarm that stretched
beyond the music, anger even, on its behalf
and ours, but still he held the note
and still the cries accompanied it, insistent,
shrill, a caterwaul crescendo
overwhelming everything. But then
the father recognised its source,

and love, embarrassment, ambiguous
apology sealed up his eyes again
in a transcendental smile. He knew
as we did that this was inescapably the music
of what happens, that what happens
is part of the design.
                                And so the performance
closed with our applause and laughter,
understanding and complicity. Then
as we left the church, united
in a different light, we passed
the mother and her twins
illuminated by it too, for that moment
witnessing their own epiphany,
how it would be recalled like this
how that mischievous divine intent
had done its work, renewed the score
for all of us, a mother
and a father written into it, their children
yet to learn the part they'd played
although already like two grace notes
held together, falling back to sleep.

ACROSS THE WORLD

How vulnerable our little gatherings
to a change in the weather, how suddenly
wind and rain gather their strength outside
and then become an inner howl
that breaks the glass. A full moon's face
is at the window, its drenched reflection
inconsolable, not begging to come in
but here already as of right, pale as death
from across the world, to warm itself
beside a fire so lovingly built up
where ash and flickering residual flames
lay waste the crumbs of comfort.

However we arrange our china plates
they cannot hide a fault line
opening across the table, however
we spread the cloth a tremor
lifts it. Our fragile, ritual domesticities
will not protect us from the towering
wave of conscience or the tide
that swells as it recedes and carries
everything we thought was ours alone
toward oblivion. So happiness is luck
and loss no less the possibility
that what may never happen surely does.

THE GESTURE

To step forward to the canvas then back from it
without making a mark, and to do this
again and again as the paint on the brush
thickens, as my eye, my hand, my heart
refuse to repeat the gesture once made freely
with a synthesis of joy. What Auerbach called
the safety net of manner could be mine
if I admitted it, to break my fall and rest there
saved by repetition. What you might say
is 'Nobody paints like him, amazingly prolific
for his age, such energy, such vision', easy words
like that, but exactly so, I should indeed
be nobody with nothing left to show but a blank
and vacuous deception. No, I'm not ready yet.

THE COUNTERPOINT

Momentum, melody, miraculous surprise
of wordless utterance rings out
the changes as we sound them
reaching for analogies. How each note
marked by time and keeping it becomes
a pilgrim shaking off the burden
of unanswered prayer. Or suddenly,
its deep breath liberally exhaled,
draws music from the well where echoes
gather in anticipation, joining
to begin a song, familiar though
never before so clear, the counterpoint
of loss accepted and the gift of grace.

BLACK'S MEDICAL DICTIONARY

Waiting for test results
I recall my father's bookshelf
and the embossed gilt spine
of *Black's Medical Dictionary.*

How I would take it down
when no one was around
to find the condition
that matched each new ache.

Compulsive connoisseur
of my growing pains,
there was no condition
I didn't have.

If I bent an arm,
if I stretched out a leg,
the shadow of death
was suddenly cast

by this or that symptom
or sinister virus
that would carry me off
before my time.

Page upon page
was an exquisite terror,
a glimpse of the dark
through light of day.

Now going online
is an open secret,
far too much choice
for a credulous man

who recalls where his father
placed fear on the shelf
between *Practical Accounting*
and *Birds of Great Britain.*

SCAN

I shall be radioactive
for eight hours afterward
and must be careful
to avoid intimate contact.
The prospect of this
alarms me, but what now
suddenly comes to mind
is just how alone I felt
standing in Hereford Cathedral
October 1962
beside the Mappa Mundi
with Khrushchev banging on
as nuclear war seemed
unavoidable, that the world
could soon be dust, this sacred
storehouse of humanity
and faith be flattened
in an instant. Eight hours
or not much more
was all I'd have to hurry home
before our precious intimacy
would vanish in the void
and love, left echoing,
become an empty word.

CONVALESCENCE

Walking to the end of the garden
is a short distance and after such heavy rain
I can't be heavy-hearted. Everything
glistens as the sun returns, is resolutely
not bowed down but reaches up
and outward with a playful generosity
of water. I brush against the burgeoning
jasmine bush we planted. Sure enough
it turns its sprinkler on and drenches me
like loving in a shower. Soon, it says
or seems to, you'll be doing that again
and chuckles as I pass. Already
I'm laughing aloud at how absurd
and wet and happy I feel. I should
of course go in, dry off, warm up,
be sensible but not just yet. Not yet.

ADVENTURE

Our next-door neighbours' Burmese cat
let out to explore is hanging by his claws
to the guttering. A Tom and Jerry situation
or a Hitchcock? Anthropomorphic either way.
Adventure is the wide world all before him,
learning by suspense, no safety net,
no garden seat to watch from as I do
in my cosseted, retiring zone of comfort
wondering what next, and making little verses
out of risk by proxy, under my breath
admiringly to call out Go, cat, Go!

THE SWING OF THINGS

How to get back in the swing of things
when things are not as they were
is a problem with language: too many verbs
in search of nouns, rejected adjectives
jostling for attention, no subject
worth their eager expenditure. Line
by line by line, the past repeats itself
like a conman caught in the act
of his next transaction. Oh to go straight,
no longer the receiver of a suitcase
packed with used notes but a neophyte
of promise printing his own currency
crisp, fresh-minted, starting all over
as himself alone. What's done is done
and if it lives must take its chances
in a world elsewhere and sign the paper
with another hand, the mere compliance
of a stranger on parole. Read it if you will
but here, now, from the cell of language
I release myself in the first person
to a sentence that begins without me,
a future tense to take the poem
where it will, with luck to bring me back
into the swing of things and lead me on.

FRAILTIES

HOW ALL OCCASIONS

Let me wipe it first, said Lear
When Gloucester knelt
To kiss his hand, *it smells*
Of mortality. Such lines
Too readily surprise me
As I stumble into age
Supported by quotation.

Like just now, in a subterranean
Gents, holding my hands
Under the dryer, their skin
A septuagenarian blur
Of ripple and flap
As they rode the blasting
Downward current of warm air.

GAMMY

My brain gives marching orders
And my legs obey,
The left one performing
A theatrical limp
As tentative unsteadiness
Accelerates to lope.

The right propels,
 Supporting a weight
That certainly needs attention,
 But am I not a character
The way I get along,
 Raising my hat to passers-by.

SHAGGY DOG

Do I repeat myself?
Very well then, I repeat myself
As Whitman very nearly said
But didn't, though he might have
Had he lived a little longer
Than his last attenuated lines
Or his beard at seventy-three.

Who was it said that he planned
To erect a statue to amnesia
Then forget where he put it?
Listen, I heard this yesterday
And shall no doubt tell you again tomorrow.
Thus does the terminal shaggy dog
Jump up and wag its tail.

BEFORE THE FALL

Only a matter of time now
Before I miss my footing, fall
On the washed steps of a urinal
Or in the aisle at Tesco,
Staring at a white tiled wall
Or stacked shelves, row upon row.

Slow-burn bruise, cracked
Rib, the unavoidable paradigm
Of our future, yours and mine,
For the longer we stay intact
It's only a matter of time
Just as time is a matter of fact.

ON THE MENU

Misreading on the menu
Apricot Soufflé
As Apricot Shuffle,
I dance to the music
Of transposition
And ocular delight

As here begin the inventive
Pleasures of short sight
To compensate
For all those longer
Desserts of Vast Eternity
That lie ahead.

5 A.M.

My emotional satnav
Recalculates as I wake
From a rough night's journey
In the wrong direction.
It sounds determined
To set me on my feet.

But not yet. An old-style
Finger-pointing map-reader,
I stare at the ceiling
And blank out that inner voice,
Its lack of confidence
In how my days take shape.

MISTAKEN

Looking out on a morning mist
Which at first I take
To be thick, familiar fog,
My heaviness of heart
Is ready to resume
Another dark, unlifted day,

Until, rising to meet
The sun's unexpected
Breakthrough, I seem to
Walk on air. Do they mark
My departure or arrival,
These footsteps in moist grass?

ALONE

Walking alone in the garden
I call a neighbour's cat to my side,
Having lost our own.
He shrugs his fur,
Turns deliberately away
And leaps back over the fence.

Nothing personal, old man,
But the way you look at me
Smacks of a neediness
My nature can't address.
Like you, like Kipling's cat,
I too must walk alone.

SAFE JOURNEY

In Clouzot's *The Wages of Fear*
Yves Montand drives home
On a mountain road,
Dangerously elated
To have survived
The delivery of nitroglycerine.
He waltzes his emptied truck
To strains of *The Blue Danube*.

Too late he sees a car approach
And swerves in earnest,
Plunging to his death.
I think of this as I too
Drive home, inwardly
Elated by hospital good news
But, always a prudent driver,
Signalling each move.

THE TRICK

Too late for fruit,
Too soon for flowers.
The bedside wit
Of Walter de la Mare
As he struggled to greet
His anxious visitors,

To perform the trick
Of one last
Playful, melancholic,
Typical jest.
Then *But yes, I* **am** *sick*
I'm afraid, he confessed.

CHEER UP

I dwell far too much
On the inescapable
As if already signed up
To my ageing body's
Mortal manifesto.

So I reassure myself
That there's work to do
While the heart still beats
And the bright blood flows
Through every sunlit vein.

ON A LINE FROM SKELTON

My words hang together
Like feathers in the wind.
Entirely by chance
They brush against each other
And for a moment hold.

More often, though,
Like a light snowfall,
Theirs is the solitary
Drift to an earth
That soon absorbs them.

THE ANSWER

Here at the cliff's edge
I have come to stand on
With a deadweight of grief
Pressing me forward
I ask myself over and over
What is there to lose?

And the answer is everything
That we did together,
Not to be betrayed by
Forgetting it now
As I scan the horizon
Then step back for a better view.

IN TWO MINDS

Staring into an empty
Wine glass, and wondering
Whether or not
To pour another,
I tell myself to let the bottle
Make the decision for me.

I pinch the glass's stem
With a gardener's tenderness
As if to replant the bloom
In a richer soil, and wait
For its resurrection
When the sun comes out.

IN THE BAG

My nerves seem nervous
Of each other. They jostle
In the bag and introduce themselves
Like guests at a party
Invited to make up numbers,
Already eager to leave.

Assuming I'm their host,
They can't avoid me
Since my bewilderment
Is the reason they came.
So circulate, I tell them,
And treat this as your home.

OLD BUFFER

As I stumble with misdirection
In a room full of expletives,
They come at me, the four-letter
Copulatives and defecations,
Ambushing each false move.

No one to blame but myself,
I acknowledge their right
To make a fool of me,
Leaping monosyllabically
From the thickets of age.

LOOSE ENDS

So many loose ends
That get looser
Every time they come at me
With their multiplying
Frayed reminders.

All not fully done
Or left undone
As this paralysing
Welter of indecision
Strikes when least expected.

CSL

(Magdalene College 1962)

I remember the Professor
Sitting rigid under a tree
In the Fellows Garden
Staring at nothing
But the vacancy of his bereavement
Not to be disturbed.

It seemed to me then
Such a long way off,
That the dead must belong
To another country
And that dreaming of Narnia
Might pass the time.

INSTRUCTED

One bird remains now
To peck at the feeder,
And a last leaf
Hangs from the thread
Of a broken web.

I share with them
This image of myself,
A stubborn tenacity,
Residual, inherited,
Or so the poem tells me.

A LITTLE ILLNESS

Fearing my imagination's
Lack of drive, its indifference
To yet another poem's
Arrival or departure,
I begin to understand
The anxious artist in his prime

Who said 'I always keep
A little illness in reserve'
And drew on it ambiguously
When with hesitant concern
His friends would ask him
Whether a loan might help.

THE NEXT ROOM

The laughter now is always
In the next room, yours
And mine as it was,
While I sit here reminiscently
Alone, catching the drift
If not the words, then
Writing us back together.

To do this is to find that room,
Turning the light back on,
And there we are once more,
Our chairs no longer empty,
With so much to say to each other
That it will be some time
Before I have to leave.

SO FAR

Early evening sun
Pours into this wine glass
A solitary consolation.
I pluck the stem
And raise its blossom
Half-way to my lips

Then pause to admire
The blazing varieties of green
As they fill our garden
With a light so far from dying
In the breeze's animation
That the best seems yet to come.

CIRCUMSTANCES

To Mary

*

And did you get what
you wanted from this life, even so?
I did.
And what did you want?
To call myself beloved, to feel myself
beloved on the earth.
– Raymond Carver

I HEAR YOU CALLING ME

That sentimental Irish song,
Count John McCormack's signature,
Plays on my mind while talking
With our neighbour. His wife died
More than a year ago
But I still hear her at night
Calling me to come and help.

How the dead
Must press against the living
And the living acquiesce
In preparation. Now my wife
Alone in the room
Where once the two of us
Slept soundly calls me
On bad nights to settle her,
Adjust the bedclothes,
Offer what help I can.

Often, awake
And apprehensive, I mistake
The shift of my own body
For her voice and rise
To find her sleeping
Just as we always did
Together, a discovery
Not without pain
Yet checked by a redemptive
Sense of the ridiculous,
As some of us in growing old
Find sentimental songs

Can set us weeping
Against all reason
Before we find ourselves
Caught short by laughter.

SOME DREAMS

Some dreams you wake from
On a thread that pulls you back
To the point where nothing happened
But all turned sour. From there
A stain spread, clouding the day
You rise to now. Better be upright
With tasks to perform,
Letting routine resume
Its loosening forgetfulness,
Snapping the thread
Into a broken necklace
As beads spill sweetly
Not to be restrung.

TRYST

I help you upstairs each tyrannous
Early evening when your back
Gives out and only lying flat
Can give relief. We switch on
Classic FM and a muted angle-poise
On its shelf above the bed.
You close your eyes, shifting
Into a good position, sigh,
Then ask me to stay up for a while
And listen to the music.

                Sitting beside you
I'm watchful, ready
For that moment
When your body rises ghostly
From its palpable self,
Diaphanous, to leave
A sleeping effigy still
Lying there. Nothing could seem
More natural, as if some tryst
Has been arranged without
Our knowing, a secrecy
Of resurrection kept
Until now for us.

                So though you lie there
I have met you here
And we are holding hands
As we did at first, setting out
Unhobbled, pain-free
In our prime, and laughing
At all those little things
We'd always notice
With a lifetime yet to share.

THE SONG

I would write words
For the song you tried to teach me
Humming it in snatches
Saying *It goes something like this*
Which is all I can remember,
Since when your forgetfulness
Has been a gift as precious
As that summer afternoon,
Its long grass lying
Printed where we lay,
Our laughter a notation
Carrying on the breeze
In search of what might still
Return to us, reclaimed
And set to music
With such words as these.

REMISSION

I live through your pain
With love, and celebrate
Each second of relief
In hope that something
Miraculous may happen,
That intimacy's thief
Will not break through again,

And I recall the thrill
Of entering our first home
Together, not on lease
But in full possession,
When you turned with a smile
That lit up your face
For a long, long while.

PROCEDURE

From separate rooms, the landing light
Left on, safe passage
For anxieties and apprehensions,
You call out or I hear you breathing
Steadily enough to let me
Snatch at sleep, but never deep enough
To find the dark, to lie there
Beyond interruption.
                         Come dawn,
The light dissolves in light,
The paper's clattering delivery
By old Michael on his scooter
With its whiny electric stop-and-start
And reassuring hum is where
Full consciousness begins.

                              Then
Time for what we call the procedure
Starting with my shower,
Via medication, clothing choice
And spoon-fed breakfast
Down to your special chair
As after forty seven years
This now becomes our story's
Opening paragraph, the prologue
To another day of patience,
Anger, watchfulness and love.

SPECTRAL MISCHIEF

Ghosts that pass through walls
Are no less palpable
Than either of us seated

In the confines of this room
From which escape
Might be a spectral mischief,

A trick to play on the world
We were so willingly a part of
Until it took its leave of you,

Appointing me companion
To your slow abandonment
Consoled by thoughts like these.

GETTING ON WITH THINGS

The length of the morning in the one chair
At an awkward angle but to disturb you there
Would be to interrupt a spell of comfort
Which looks like sleep. You insist that it's not.
It's just that I have my eyes closed
When I'm like this. I need the rest
And, besides, you worry too much.
Get on with things. I'll be all right.

So another domestic day to fetch
And carry, to watch and wait
Between helping you to dress
In freshly-washed clothes
And seeing you to an early bed,
With windows of conversation opened
When the drugs allow, mealtimes
With your bent spoon, a short walk
On my arm the length of the street
If you're steady enough
And all this through another day of love
Proved, I hope, not by muddled talk
But by getting on with things.

TISSUE

You sit with it plucked
From the box at your feet,
Held at a distance,
Surprised to find it there
Like waving goodbye.

I take it from you
And wipe your mouth
As at first you intended,
The little white flag
That you surrender.

THE GAP

The gap, not being exactly
Silence but your answer
On hold, is time enough
For the guilt of my impatience
To find its edge, to cut
To the quick of irritation
Then find the words
That might for a moment
Speak for both of us.

I sit beside you now,
Your baffled, tentative
Amanuensis, adrift
In the neverland
Of what you want to say
But brought to this halt
By mutual misdirection,
Lost in the gap between us
As we wait for it to close.

AERIAL

Aero modeling took hours of patience
As the fuselage and then the wings
Revealed a skeletal shape
That had found its place; brittle, tense,
And ready for the papery skin
To be tightened overnight with dope.

Next morning, lifting it from the table,
Holding it up, imagining flight,
I'd perform a special manoeuvre
That memory now makes palpable
As I help you out of bed, your featherweight
But earthbound body entrusted to my care.

BREATH

Your breath cuts out like that V1
Above the stage outside a hospital
For the wounded in a scene
From *The Glenn Miller Story*
Where the band goes on playing
While everyone else ducks down
For cover then, when from elsewhere
The explosion comes, stands up
Applauding, roaring
With admiration and relief.

Just, or almost, so it is
As I lie here in this separate bed
Beside you, and your open-mouthed
Gargling snore suddenly closes
On silence. Although I know
It will soon resume, in this case
Thankfully not elsewhere, my dark thoughts
Duck for cover, even as life
Plays on, until they can breathe again
And silently applaud.

WINTER GARDEN

Our forsythia bush shoots up
Its sparsely golden branches
Like Shock-Headed Peter's hair
As a colony of sparrows
Zinging back and forth
Takes off, returns, keeps swinging there.

Any branch unvisited, bereft,
Will soon be chosen
To bend, companionably sway
And bear its little weight
In this relief from loneliness
Making my day.

FISHERMAN'S WHARF

Just married, forty five years ago
Exploring San Francisco,
You in your poppy-red coat, my camera
Aimed across the water
At Alcatraz, we were side by side, then,
Laughing, all of a sudden
You ran ahead. Turning to wave back at me,
It was as if you had intended to say
Don't just stand there, come on.
This is our happiness. Join in.

I was so in love with how you ran
From me, knowing you would turn
Like that, and even now the bright
Passionate kiss of your coat
Despite its bleached surroundings
Has not faded, though while I sit watching
This treasured, antique home movie
Without you it's as if already
You had known what I still can't say
And were waving goodbye.

THE RUG

Spread out across sand
Or shingle with a hamper's
Lunchtime bounty, sandwiches
Of sliced tomato, hard-boiled egg
And grated cheese, to lie back on it
After paddling, to feel the sun's warmth
Move across your face, to hear
A shrill delight of cries and laughter
All around, and further off
The surfing come-and-go
Of summer waves.

Spread out now across your knees
Beside the fire and holding in
A necessary comfortable
Winter warmth, it still recaptures
Sunlight, how the sand-grains
Sparkled in its weave, how rolled up
On the car's back seat
It journeyed home through time
Toward this memory of happiness
And no less a good companion
Than it always was,

THE KISS

One kiss to wake her
Hacking through brambles
To the bridal bed
Then after consummation
Back to where they were
In the glorious
Thick of life
With nothing changed
Or withered. So
The story goes
Which is not our story,
Nor can the kiss
I give you now
Be one to rouse us both
As back then
It might have done
But, given softly
On dry lips in hope
To make you smile,
It may yet help the two of us
To settle down and sleep.

HANG ON

The wisteria leaves are hanging on,
Sere and yellow. Even the wind
Can do nothing about it. This
Should be a time for pruning
But there's something in their
Up-against-the-wall tenacity
That won't let go.
                              Overnight
No doubt they will succumb
To frost or weariness,
Shedding the burden
Of their frail outlasting
Soon enough,
But until that time
Let them be our emblem
As we negotiate each day.
Hang on, my love, hang on.

WIDOWER

Weary of his eagerness
Their eyes glaze over,
The darkness of a conversation
Helplessly one-sided,
Driven by a search for light.

Just someone to talk to
In lieu of the response
Which once would have been
So naturally forthcoming
Without a second thought.

THAW

I stare at this blank page until my eyes hurt
And words lie buried, locked in ice
Beneath deep snow, but then the thought of you

Is lamplight on a dark field, every grassblade
Warming to your touch as memories
Retrace the onward journey of our love.